Incas

A Comprehensive Look at the Largest Empire in the Americas

Eric Brown

© Copyright 2018 by Eric Brown

All rights reserved.

The following eBook is reproduced below with the goal of providing information that is as accurate and reliable as possible. Regardless, purchasing this eBook can be seen as consent to the fact that both the publisher and the author of this book are in no way experts on the topics discussed within and that any recommendations or suggestions that are made herein are for entertainment purposes only. Professionals should be consulted as needed prior to undertaking any of the action endorsed herein.

This declaration is deemed fair and valid by both the American Bar Association and the Committee of Publishers Association and is legally binding throughout the United States.

Furthermore, the transmission, duplication or reproduction of any of the following work including specific information will be considered an illegal act irrespective of if it is done electronically or in print. This extends to creating a secondary or tertiary copy of the work or a recorded copy and is only allowed with an expressed written consent from the Publisher. All additional rights reserved.

The information in the following pages is broadly considered to be a truthful and accurate account of facts, and as such any inattention, use or misuse of the information in question by the reader will render any resulting actions solely under their purview. There are no scenarios in which the publisher or the original author of this work can be in any fashion deemed liable for any hardship or damages that may befall them after undertaking information described herein.

Additionally, the information in the following pages is intended only for informational purposes and should thus be thought of as universal. As befitting its nature, it is presented without assurance regarding its prolonged validity or interim quality. Trademarks that are mentioned are done without written consent and can in no way be considered an endorsement from the trademark holder.

Table of Contents

Introduction 5

Chapter 1: Seeds of an Empire 7

Chapter 2: A Difficult Place to Live....................................... 15

Chapter 3: A Day in the Life.. 21

Chapter 4: The Gods.. 34

Chapter 5: Decline and Downfall.. 44

Chapter 6: Remains of the Day 53

Conclusion.. 59

Introduction

When the conversation begins about the great civilizations of the Americas, there are three general that come to mind: the Mayans, the Aztecs, and the Incas. But while the Mayans and the Aztecs were similar in their cultures and geographically very close together, the Inca Empire was separate both by land and social structure. Because of these assumptions made, much of what is 'known' about the Inca Empire is actually misattributed from these perceived connections.

The Inca Empire covered the Andes mountain range in South America, covering today what is Peru and Chile. They flourished for over 200 years, quickly becoming the largest and most powerful region in the Americas before their potential was tragically cut short by the invading Spaniards. Today, not much remains of the great Inca but ruins of their cities and whispers of their legacy.

Or, is there? After all, just because your high school history class never talked about it, doesn't mean the information isn't out there. In fact, we have more knowledge pertaining to the Inca Empire than we do on either the Mayans or the Aztecs, perhaps even combined.

In the following pages, you will learn all you need to know to shock friends and family with your knowledge of Inca culture and history. From the foundations of their empire to their impractical geological location, and how they managed to flourish despite the odds. Customs and social structure, government and politics, and the lives of citizens. Religion and warfare. Everything culminating with the Inca's downfall at the hands of Columbus and his disease-ridden, death-mongering conquerors.

In fact, by the time you've finished this book, you may be ready to school your teachers.

Chapter 1: Seeds of an Empire

The Inca Empire did not actually form until sometime in the 1200s, making it younger than the University of Oxford. However, this does not mean that the area was uninhabited or entirely primitive. The indigenous people of the Andes mountain range lived for thousands of years prior to this, untouched and undisturbed.

Scholars referred to these people as 'pristine,' meaning they were untouched by any neighboring indigenous people. The Andeans developed their own languages and ways of communication. The primary language used was Quechua, which would later go on to be the official language of the Incan Empire. Notably, the Andeans had no written language. Nor were they an oral society, like most other American indigenous groups. Instead, information was conveyed through something called the 'quipu,' a series of intricately knotted and color-coded strings. Fascinating though they are, there are few left in existence, and no one has ever been able to decipher a quipu. Whatever information is recorded in those strings, we will likely never know.

Andean people are also notable for never developing the wheel. The rocky, uneven terrain of their homeland makes this development understandable, however, as a wheel could prove anything from a hindrance to useless. Instead, Andeans used llamas as pack animals, and before the empire, they rarely traveled.

An impact the Andean civilizations had that lasted through the Incan Empire was their lack of currency. Instead, they existed on a system of reciprocity, distributing goods and services in exchange for labor.

The Tiwanaku
In Bolivia, where the city-state of Tiwanaku was situated, a civilization lasted hundreds of years and predated the Incas by almost two centuries. Ranging from about 300-1150 CE, they expanded their reach through politics and trade, but their downfall came at the hands of climate change, as was so often the case in such an area.

The Wari
Neighbors of the Tiwanaku, the Wari civilization formed around 600 BCE. A wealthy people, with its own administrative structure, they co-existed peacefully with the Tiwanaku for centuries. The Wari civilization lasted until the same climate change caused their crops to fail, and their power structures began to crumble. In the time that passed after those two small empires saw their fall, a new power was beginning to grow.

Kingdom of Cusco
The semi-legendary figure of Manco Capac began life as a nomad, a wanderer of the mountains. With his small tribe, he found the Huatanay valley high in the Andes. The area was only mildly settled by other small tribes, and so Manco Capac settled his family and turned the area into the city we know as Cusco.

Because of the lack of written records, it's hard to know just what of Manco Capac's life was real and what was a mere myth. Legend says he founded the city of Cusco itself, but history shows us that the valley was already well occupied and the city was a small but thriving area. How much Manco Capac did to found Cusco doesn't matter so much as what he did afterward, however, as it was under his leadership that the city turned from a mere settlement into a kingdom. He abolished the local practice of human sacrifice, and set new laws and administration in place. The city expanded, new buildings included a stone palace where he and his family lived.

In the native language of the Incas, Quechua, the kingdom was named 'Qosco.' This makes it notable among Spanish-conquered cities for having retained its native name, and not be given a new, Catholic name. 'Qosco' in Quechua means 'center.' This name would mark its importance as the center of the future Inca Empire.

Manco Capac reigned for forty years and died peacefully. His son, Sinchi Ruq'a, took up the mantle after him, establishing a dynasty that would last for generations. Leaders of the Kingdom of Cusco would take the title 'Sapa Inca.' The ninth of these men, a great visionary named Pachacuti, would expand the kingdom even further.

Pachacuti was not born with this name, it was given to him to describe his great deeds. Born as Cusi Yupanqui, he was a younger brother and not even meant to inherit the title of Sapa Inca. But when he was a young man, Cusco fell under siege to a neighboring tribe, the Chankas. While his father and brother fled, Cusi Yupanqui faced his enemies head-on. He fought so fiercely, those who witnessed the battle said even the stones raised themselves from their sleep to fight alongside him. It was because of this event that he was given the new name Pachacuti, which means 'Earth Shaker.' He was named Sapa Inca, for his true loyalty to Cusco had shone while his cowardly family hid away.

But Pachacuti was not content to remain. He expanded Cusco in all directions, bringing all surrounding tribes under his rule. By his death, the Kingdom of Cusco was twice the size of what it had been. In the twenty years of his son's reign, it had doubled again. It is during this frame of time that the Kingdom of Cusco became what we know today as the Inca Empire, and it would only continue to grow and expand.

The Four Nations
The Incan Empire, during the height of its glory, was divided into four sub-kingdoms, like territories. Each of these quarters was grouped due to the previous tribes that had existed and had control of the land, before the Incan expansion. The Incas, a little like the Romans, chose to absorb rather than conquer.

Each of these territories was given the suffix –suyu, which in Quechua means 'region.' The prefix of their name was usually attributed to the direction of the province, and the Quechua names for the natives living in that area. Government administration meant that these regions still maintained a level of autonomy within the empire.

Chinchasuyu was the northernmost province. The name comes from the Chincha culture, a trader kingdom that occupied the area. 'Chincha' is also a word that, in Quechua, means 'north,' denoting the direction. The region stretches into the Peruvian deserts and was one of the larger quarters.

Antisuyu was the eastern province. 'Anti' was the Quechua name for the people living here, and also means 'east.' The borders of Antisuyu reached into the edges of the Amazon jungle. 'Anti' is also the root word from which our name for the mountains, 'Andes,' takes its name. Because of contact with the

Amazon, Antisuyu was the empire's doorway into the rainforests vast resources like cocoa and gold.

Kuntisuyu was the western province. 'Kunti' means west. It was the smallest of the four. It also covered a portion of Peru, including the deserts, and the area of Nazca – famous today for the Nazca lines. The steep drop to the coast meant that many important resources from the sea came from this region, and were distributed outward.

Qullasuyu was the southern and largest of the four quarters. 'Qulla' means 'south,' and stretched down the Andes into today's Chile and Bolivia. The mostly grassland region was home to the empire's agricultural center, and home to hers of llamas and alpacas.

All four of these provinces converged in Cusco, making it truly the center of the Incan world. Together, they were known as Tawantinsuyu, meaning 'The Four Regions.'

Growing Strong
Pachacuti, despite his early military success, chose instead to expand his reach by politics and peace. He had an adept network of spies, who could infiltrate the small, neighboring kingdoms and take inventory of their armies and wealth, their haves, and their needs. Pachacuti would then appeal to the leaders of these kingdoms, extolling the virtues and benefits of his empire, and how great it would profit to join him. This effective method gave Pachacuti all the advantages of expansion, without expending resources.

This also meant that the Incan Empire was a mosaic people. Although Quechua was the official language, there were almost a dozen smaller local languages. The empire was connected by roads and trade flourished.

Foundation Myth

There is a foundation myth of the Inca Empire. Just as every civilization has a story of their first founding, the Inca story is full of magic and religion and not at all historically accurate. But understanding the Incans own beliefs as to where they originated can help understand them better as a people.

Once, before the days of the Empire, when the people of Cusco were nothing but herders and farmers, there were three caves deep in the mountains. The center cave was named Qhapaq T'uqu. The caves on its left and right were named Maras T'uqu and Sutiq T'uqu.

One day, from out of the central cave, eight humans stepped out into the sun. Four brothers, named Ayar Manco, Ayar Cachi, Ayar Awqa and Ayar Uchu. They were joined by four sisters, who went by the names Mama Ocllo, Mama Raua, Mama Huaco and Mama Qura.

The eldest brother, Ayar Manco, carried a staff made of solid gold. Imbued with magic powers, this staff would bring life wherever it struck the ground. The four brothers and four sisters traveled a long way, leaving life behind them in a trail of flourishing green.

Of the four brothers, one got on everyone's nerves more than the rest. This was Ayar Cachi, the second-eldest. He had a big mouth, constantly talking about his own great power when he was not the one who held the magic staff. Finally, the traveling companions tired of him. So they used flattery to trick him into returning to Qhapaq T'uqu, the cave from whence they came.

Inside is a sacred llama, they promised, and only you have enough great power to retrieve it. A smart man would have known not to look for a llama in a cave, but Ayar Cachi fell victim to his own ego. Once inside the cave, his brothers sealed him inside and were effectively rid of him.

But in the time that had passed since the siblings left the caves, more people had begun to come from the caves on the left and right. These people are said to be the first Incas, and all further generations can trace their lineage back to these people. The youngest brother, Ayar Uchu, decided he would remain at the caves and watch over these people. So he climbed atop the cave and made a proclamation to look after and care for them. As he said it, he turned to stone, an ever-present guardian.

Ayar Auca, the third brother, decided he was tired of his family's antics. So he turned his back and went to wander alone. Ayar Manco and the four sisters were all that remained. They built a shrine around their petrified brother and then continued on their travels.

As they wandered, Ayar Manco and Mama Ocllo fell in love. They had a child together, a son named Sinchi Ruq'a. After his birth, the travelers came across the small city of Cusco. Deciding that this would be their home, Ayar Manco placed his magical golden staff into the ground.

Cusco was, at this point in time, occupied by small tribes. They did not want Ayar Manco and his companions to take their land and fought hard against the invaders. But one of the sisters, Mama Huaco, stepped up to the plate. She tied several stones together and flung them through the air, creating a staple weapon of the Incas known as bolas. The bolas hit one of the fighters, and he was instantly struck down. In fear and awe of this woman's incredible capabilities, the people of Cusco turned and ran.

From that moment on, Ayar Manco went by the name Manco Capac, and the rest is history. This legend says that he founded the Inca, rather than simply turning Cusco into a small kingdom. Whereas the real Manco Capac died peacefully in his sleep, according to legend, he turned to stone upon his deathbed like his brother.

Chapter 2: A Difficult Place to Live

Apart from the Inca Empire, no civilization has ever built itself around and atop a mountain range. Because no civilization could ever figure out how to survive on one. A mountainous race is reserved for fantasy worlds, where authors can create fictional mountain ranges filled with riches to make up for other hardships or have them populated by nonhumans entirely.

But the Incas were not Tolkien dwarves, and yet they managed to survive. Not only that, but they managed to thrive in a hostile environment. And the way they did this may seem like something out of a fantasy novel itself.

First, we need to understand the geography. At the height of its power, the Incan Empire ranged from modern Ecuador to almost the bottom of Chile. Though it did stretch itself into Bolivia and Argentina, the Incas are notable for having for length north to south than they do east to west.

The Mountains

So, why choose to stay centralized around the highest mountain range in the Western Hemisphere? After all, the Andes seem like the last choice for a settlement. Not only do they reach dangerous altitudes of 6,900 meters (over 22,000 feet) but they are part of the Pacific Ring of Fire. Volcanoes are abundant along the range.

The Andes are also famous for their varied and unpredictable weather. There are three entirely different climates found along the range: wet, dry, and tropical. In all three of these climates, air pressure and temperature drop drastically the higher you climb, and the snow line – that is, the elevation at which snowfall begins to occur – is variant depending on location.

The Wet Andes is the southernmost part of the range, reaching all the way to Cape Horn at the bottom tip of South America. They have a high rainfall and cold temperatures, meaning most of it is covered in glaciers. There is little to no plant life, making it nigh inhospitable for human settlements.

The Dry Andes takes up most of the middle of the mountains and has a semiarid desert climate. This means that it suffers through low precipitation and a lack of vegetation. The only flora to grow is stubbly, such as grass or shrubs. Like deserts, semiarid landscapes are known for hot days and cold nights. On top of this, there are several glaciers situated in the mountains, some reaching close to 10 km (6 miles) in length.

Finally, the Tropical Andes is the largest and northernmost portion. There are high peaks, valleys, and canyons, all covered in forests. The type of forest changes as the elevation gets higher. At its lowest point, the Tropical Andes is a tropical rainforest, with very high precipitation and is always hot. As the tree climb higher, they become a cloud forest. These rainforests can be easily visualized by their name alone: it is a forest, and it is cloudy. High temperatures combined with closer cloud cover means the area is densely foggy, and the natural evolution of the trees has made them gnarled and hunched over. Everything about cloud forests gives them an otherworldly, ethereal look. Finally, at its highest points, the Tropical Andes resemble something closer to the Dry Andes, with a steppe climate.

With so many rapid changes in weather and climate, most other budding civilizations would have packed up and left to find another home. So why didn't the Incas? The area provided uncomfortable living conditions and a lack of area for farming and agriculture. Were they just so stubborn that they refused to leave? The truth is, perhaps they might have tried to migrate. But any direction they could have gone in would create just as many problems.

The Deserts
Where the Andes end, up in Peru, the coastline is an arid desert. The conditions are much more extreme than those found in the Dry Andes, with temperatures of 35 Celsius (95 Fahrenheit) on a normal day. Near the southwest Andes, too, is a desert stretch, in modern-day southern Argentina. But these areas were not uninhabited, and Peru especially had several thriving cultures before the Incas were founded. The Moche, the Nazca, and the Norte Chico civilization all lived in the deserts and saw no reason to migrate away from their hot homeland.

The Jungle
Any climb down the Andes, if it didn't lead to a desert, it led to a jungle. South America is known for its tropical rainforests, most famously the Amazon that stretches across Brazil to Bolivia. Like the jungles covering the Tropical Andes, the humidity is stifling. But the tropical rainforest has the added bonus of predators. The Amazon itself is home to jaguars, anacondas, piranhas, on top of a variety of poisonous bugs and amphibians. Most tribes inhabiting the jungle remained small and contained, even to this day.

And so, with all the problems facing the early Inca, the question seems not to be 'Why?' but 'Why not?' Like the

Peruvian desert peoples and the jungle tribes, the Inca had no better chance of surviving in a new climate than they did in their own. Anywhere else they could go seemed just as frustratingly complicated. And so the Inca did what mankind is best known for: they adapted.

Ecological Adaptations

One of the most primary farming adaptations made by the Andean people was to plant crops at several different elevations. By doing this, they could test the variables of weather, altitude, and soil quality. When it came to cultivating food, the main staple of the Andean diet was squash. Because the fruit has a thick skin and grows better in harsher climates, squash was popular all over the Americas. Alongside beans and maize, the Andean cultures were able to build a healthy and rich diet with little need for meat. Maize, which was developed by the Mayans in around 6,000 BCE in Mexico, was introduced to the continent of South America through trade.

Andean civilizations built their diets this way because there was a lack of large animals for food sources. South America had no horses, cattle, pigs or sheep. All the Andeans really had were llamas. Despite their usefulness as a meat source, llamas were also naturally very trainable animals and were equally useful as packers.

So due to these two factors, the early Andean people developed to be an agricultural-based society instead of hunting-based. This development would stick even as the Inca Empire rose to its greatest heights. And yet, it was not this alone that caused the Inca people to be so well-adapted to their environment. Just as the squash adapted to survive the high altitudes, so did the Inca.

Evolutionary Adaptations

All across the world, we see humans evolve to fit their surroundings. Levels of melanin in the skin change to protect a skin's exposure to the sun, becoming darkest in the areas around the equator. Humans that live in colder areas develop more body hair. It is the same way animals adapt to their surroundings, evolutionary traits changing to better survive the surrounding conditions.

But the Andean people should be noteworthy for their adaptations because they exhibited some of the most extreme examples:

One of the main problems faced by higher altitudes is the air pressure or lack of it. The higher you rise, the thinner the air, and so the less oxygen your body can take in. When your brain isn't receiving the amount of oxygen it needs, you feel faint or dizzy. Many hikers who travel the Andes report these conditions and travel guides advise you to take the ascent slowly because ascending too quickly can be damaging to your blood pressure.

As there is less oxygen, your heart rate increases in an attempt to get more blood flow to the brain. Thin, in turn, causes shallow breathing, which only further detriments the lack of oxygen. This is also why high altitudes can be dangerous to anyone with high blood pressure, pre-existing medical conditions, or pregnancy. And for healthy humans, sometimes the altitudes can be even worse, as more muscle mass means your body is struggling to spread oxygen all over this larger area.

But the Incan people had a lung capacity 1/3 the size of a regular human. This meant that on a normal breath, they could take in three times the amount of oxygen. Incans also developed to be shorter in stature, meaning there was less distance for blood to travel. Their heart rates were slowed, dealing with the body's insistence to increase heart rate at heights.

Incans also had more blood volume, almost 2 liters worth. This meant they had a higher count of red blood cells, and with that comes more hemoglobin. More hemoglobin meant more oxygen could be transferred from the blood into the tissue. Incas also had more capillaries, reaching more blood through more of their skin.

So with these kinds of evolutionary adaptations, it's no wonder the Incas managed to become the dominant civilization in South America. No other grouping of people across the world has developed quite so specifically to live in hostile environments. It was, quite literally, an uphill battle against nature, and the Inca Empire came out on top.

Chapter 3: A Day in the Life

Even though their main method of recording information is a lost system, we still know a surprising amount about Incan society. This has mostly to do with the stories passed down, and the art left behind. Some parts of the Incan taxing system were even adapted, albeit to a much crueler extent, by the Spaniards.

With the remaining information resources combined with years of study, historians and anthropologists have pieced together a very clear image of a day in the life of Inca Empire. Still, all of this knowledge must be taken with a grain of salt. For all their years of study, a historian could not travel back in time. Information ranges from having concrete evidence to being hypotheses and conjecture. Take, for example, historian's guess on the empire's population. Despite the Incans taking very careful census reports, they were recorded on quipus. The estimate ranges from 4 million to 38 million.

The most important thing to remember when studying Incan society is to remember how their economy worked. Unlike most of the rest of the world, Incans did not use a money-based payment system. Instead, they paid in labor. The population was contracted to work for the government, providing goods and services. In return, the government distributed those goods back to the population. This meant trade was well-regulated throughout the empire and it was part of government policy that no one would go unclothed, unsheltered, or unfed. This curious system has baffled outsiders since the first Spaniards made contact, and yet, it seems to have worked wonders for the rich empire.

Clothing

Like many cultures, clothing played an important part in signifying an Incan's status in society. The quality of the cloth and the amount of jewelry and regalia was determined by your standing.

Wool was the primary textile. This was practical, both for the temperature drops of the mountains and because of the abundance of wool-producing animals. For the common folk, llama wool was used. Alpaca was common for an upper-middle-class family. Reserved for the nobility were the finer wools of the vicuña and the guanaco, two native Andean camelids closely related to llamas and alpacas. And in the areas with higher temperatures, especially closer to the desert, it was more common to use cotton.

Woven into the textiles were a variety of beautiful patterns, which were not restricted to social rank. Although the most skilled weavers were always sent to Cusco to weave for the nobility, clothing was distributed by the government and so always came from a reliable source. The most common patterns were quilted squares, but it was also found that geometric patterns resembling the Nazca lines would be woven in, or designs of animals. Inca fabrics were bright and colorful, and sharing these rich fabrics with new territories was one way the Inca invited people to join their empire.

Men and women wore a very similar tunic, which consisted of a single piece of sleeveless fabric wrapped around the body and pinned together at the shoulder. The main difference lies in the length. Women's tunics reached down to their feet, while men's were shorter, and worn with breeches underneath. Both men and women wore woolen cloaks for extra warmth.

Since the weather could get so cold, the Incans could not rely merely on sandals as many previous civilizations had for centuries. Instead, Incan shoes were made of llama hide and fur. When sandals were worn, they too were made with llama hide.

Because the government controlled the distribution of clothing, a strange double-edged sword was created. While it did mean that no one ever went without clothing, it also meant that clothing had to be completely worn through or outgrown before new clothing was given.

Ornamentation wasn't reserved for the nobility, though they certainly had more of it. Because the Incans did not use a classic money system, metals and gemstones were not as highly valued as they became in other societies. But there were still differences that would mark the ranks of class. The most ornamentation to be found on commoners were the pins that held tunics and cloaks together. For women, these pins doubled in function as a knife to assist with household activities.

Noblemen wore a type of turban called a llawt'u. These headwraps came with tasseled fringe. Precious stones adorned the cloaks and tunics of the upper class, and the royalty would often line the edges of cloth with gold. Royalty and nobility wore feathered headdresses, and the feathers used were dependant on station.

The most extravagant example of clothing comes from the Sapa Inca, who never wore the same cloth twice. After wearing a tunic just once, it would be burned. Thus, weavers were needed to supply him constantly. One example of taxation of the Incan government was the service of a territory's best weaver. She would be brought to Cusco and set up to live in a temple with other chosen women. This was a highly honored position.

Food

Because of the vast difference in biomes, the empire covered, and the many highways and trade routes between major cultural centers, the diet of the Incans were colorful and diverse. Like all civilizations of the Americas, they rested on the three staples: maize, squash, and beans, a tradition carried down from their ancestors before the empire was founded.

But the agricultural exploits of the Incan Empire grew to include coca leaves, tomatoes, potatoes, avocado, and peanuts. Meat was primarily llama or alpaca, but fish could be brought up from the coat. Due to the distance, it needed to travel, fish was mostly dried. Alongside them would come dried seaweed. Chili peppers became an important part of their diet, so highly valued that entire dishes began to be designed around it.

Hunting was, as everything, controlled by the state. The meat went into the storehouses to be later distributed. As for what game could be hunted, guanaco and vicuña alongside several species of deer, and chinchillas were abundant in the mountains. On the coast, a variety of limpets, rays, and sharks were fishermen's targets, alongside seabirds, sea lions, and even dolphins. Nothing was off-limits for the Incan people, and they found nutrition wherever they could.

The skill of the Incan storehouses is still a marvel to this day. The 'qollqa,' built in mass amounts all across the empire, used the advantage of cool weather on hillsides. Using a combined method of drainage and ventilation, food in these storehouses could be kept for up to two years. Since the unstable climate could lead to flooding, drought, and other natural disasters, the careful rationing of this food meant the suppliers could continue to distribute food during times of famine.

Government

The Incans had an early federalist government. Each of the four regions was divided into constituents, called 'wapani.' Although the Sapa Inca was the divine leader, with a complete and total monarchy, he had an array of government officials to help him along.

Second to the emperor only was the high priest, who went by the title 'Willaq Umu.' As religion was so closely tied to affairs of state, the two worked together on every matter. Just below them was a kind of prime minister, an advisor known as the 'Inkap Rantin.' A kind of grand council existed under these three, with sixteen nobles from the various part of the empire: four from Cusco, four each from the larger regions of Chinchasuyu and Qullasuyu, and two each from the smaller regions of Kuntisuyu and Antisuyu.

Besides the council, each region had a kind of governor known as the Apu. The wapani of each region had their own sub-governors who reported to the Apu, called the Toqriqok. Beneath them even still, every wapani had an array of officers, record keepers, and functionaries who existed to maintain infrastructure.

Law was enforced, but the laws were simple. There were three primary principles that the Incas followed: do not steal, do not murder, and do not be lazy. The lawmen officiated capital punishment, meaning there was no prison or trial system. However, the degree to which punishment was dealt out depended on whom the crime was committed. Any crime against royalty or the noble class would be punished swiftly and immediately, while those against commoners could find leniency. In general, the decision rested with the local Toqriqok.

All in all, the government system of the empire remained largely uncomplicated, and yet despite the total control held by the Sapa Inca, it seems great care was taken to make sure the common folk had their voices heard. Simple, yet effective seems the way they went.

Architecture
The Incans have been subjected to conspiracy theorists in recent years, who believed their precision cut building blocks could only have been accomplished by the use of modern technology – or extraterrestrial help. But in actuality, the Incans were just quite ingenious when it came to their architecture.

Like the effectiveness of the storehouse, Incan buildings were made to sustain. Each stone was cut to fit exactly into the one below. This was accomplished by repeatedly pushing a block to the one below, and chiseling away at the places where they found resistance. These blocks squeezed together so well that even without the use of mortar to glue them together the walls held.

Given the situation of the Andes on a subduction zone, and the Pacific Ring of Fire to boot, earthquakes were quite common, and so all buildings needed to be structurally sound enough to resist. Amazingly, the techniques of Incan masonry provided just that. Walls had little to no points of stress concentration, meaning there was no weak spot that a shaking ground could exploit.

Stones were mostly limestone, with some granite, two sources that would have been abundant. Since the Incans had no wheel, these blocks needed to be transported by man or pack. It is believed that the hardworking and labor-centric lifestyle of the Incans is what led to their amazing teamwork and dedication. Though today we see ruins as being chalky white or grey-brown, back in their glory days they would have been painted an array of bright colors.

Medicine

The introduction of the coca leaf to the rest of the empire was perhaps life-changing if the people at the time did not know it. Grown naturally in the jungles of the Amazon, cultivation of the plant quickly spread across the mountains. Today, the coca might be best known for its use as the main ingredient of the drug cocaine. It is also easily recognized as one-half of a popular soda brand, Coca-Cola.

In its natural form, the coca leaf contains several natural alkaloids that stimulate the brain, chasing away fatigue and hunger. Believed to be divine in nature, consumption of the leaf was initially restricted to the upper class. But because of the hardworking nature of Inca society, chewing on the coca leaf while working became a central part of daily life. Yet, despite its connections to the cocaine drug, coca in its natural form has no addictive properties. Consumption of the leaf can be likened to today's use of caffeine to keep alert through work hours.

On top of acting as a stimulant, the coca leaf provided the Inca with a variety of medicinal purposes. It was a remedy for altitude sickness, useful for travelers from the outlands climbing to cities like Cusco. It also found use as an anesthetic, for anything from headaches to childbirth. Most notably, it was used during the surgical procedure known as trepanation.

One of the longest-lasting types of pre-modern medical procedures, trepanation is the practice of drilling a small hole in the skull to relieve fluid buildup. Although it does nothing to help migraines or epilepsy, as was believed, it was effective against head wounds or fractured skulls gained from battle.

Stages of Life
For an Incan, there were seven stages of life one passed through. These stages were equal between men and woman because Incan society was fairly equality driven. Although women were relegated to housework, their role was in no way seen as inferior, and a woman was just as valuable as a man.

The first stage of life lasted three years and covered infancy. Because of the harsh conditions of the Andes, the infant mortality rate was very high, and babies were not named until their third birthday. This stage of life was called 'Wawa.'

Ages three through seven was the stage known as 'Ignorance,' or in Quechua, 'Warma.' This ignorance was seen as something every child would overcome with growth and experience. Though some translations name this stage as 'not speaking,' it is unbelievable that a child at age 7 would not be speaking fluently.

The third stage covered the next seven years, until the age of 14. It is during this time that the stages begin to have different names for boys and girls. For boys, the development stage was called 'Thaski,' and for girls, it was 'Maqt'a.' The reason for this divergence in names is due to the roles each gender played. This was around the time education would start for boys to become hunters or farmers, and women to learn the art of running a household: cooking, childrearing, and weaving.

The stage is known as 'Sipas' for men, and 'Wayna' for women was an interesting period, defining the age of sexual maturity before marriage. The Incans are noteworthy for their lax views on sex before marriage. No degree of abstinence was expected, for men or women. There was also a high degree of fairness at work when it came to marriage. The age of marriage was usually around 20 for men and 16 for women, though neither of these was rigid laws. Marriage itself was more of a contract and not based on love. However, it was not a binding contract. After the wedding came a trial period, and if one or both participants felt it wasn't going to work between them, the marriage could be annulled with no harm done to either man or woman's reputation.

The longest stage of life, and the general all-encompassing adulthood. This began at the age of around 20 when a person was married. It lasted all the way until age 70. For men, this stage was called 'Warmi.' For women, it was 'Qhari.' As with the previous stage, the age could differ between men and women, as the age of marriage skewed younger for women than it did men.

From ages 70 to 90, the stage of life when most passed away of natural causes, men were called 'Paya' and women 'Machu.' The meaning of these titles, 'Infirmity,' indicates some level of retirement among Incan families, where the younger members would care for the elderly in their household.

Finally, if a person could live this long, there is one final term for them: 'Ruku,' an unfortunate word meaning 'decrepit.' A person would stay in this stage until their death, which usually did not take long.

Life of a Noble
Despite this insistence the society had on hard work, even to the point of having a law forbidding laziness, the nobility spent an extreme amount of time being lazy. Likely, as is the case with most class systems, the top of the pyramid didn't believe the rules applied.

Instead, most of an Inca nobleman's daily life seems dedicated to one thing: making themselves better looking. Their daily lives were filled with luxury, eating the best foods, wearing the best clothes, and piercing themselves with the finest jewelry. At the very least, a man's duties would include learning the art of war, as the Sapa Inca often went on the front lines himself, and his generals were usually members of his family. Incan noblewomen, on the other hand, seem like little more than trophy wives. Their sole function was to look pretty and bear children. Still, thanks to the Incans relative belief in equality, noblewomen's duties were not viewed as lesser to her male counterpart.

The Inca is one of the cultures who practiced cranial deformation. This is the method of tying a board to a baby's head and reshaping the skull into an elongated point. Although this practice seems particularly cruel today, it was all done in the hopes of making one more attractive. An elongated skull was a sign of nobility to the Inca, the same way weight indicated good health in various European societies. When children are young, their bones are still soft and flexible, allowing this deformation to happen. As expected, this practice caused great pain to the child, and when they grow old enough, some rejected the practice entirely.

This strange shape is also found in the crystal skulls, carvings of crystal quartz that surfaced in the 1800s and were claimed to be from pre-Columbian societies. These skulls were a complete farce, of course, one of many ruses made by to sell 'real Native artifacts' to museums and archaeologists. And it is thanks to the crystal skull that the truth of the Inca Empire – and many other pre-Columbian civilizations to boot – became clouded by modern myths and pop culture, including the popular notion that the Inca were in contact with extraterrestrial life. There is no more evidence that aliens visited the Andes than there is anywhere else in the world, which is to say, very little and all speculation. Still, the belief that the crystal skulls are real and have paranormal abilities continues to this day.

Life of a Commoner

A commoner's life was much more practical. The Incan working class lived in family units, in houses situated around a farm. Men had jobs as either a farmer, a hunter, a builder, or an artisan, while women were weavers and cooks. The large family units meant that there was always more than one person to work the family farm, and households could include a variety of workers.

A type of conscription existed, taking one boy from every family to join the army, and one girl to be a weaver in the capital. This was not to say that multiple sons from a family could join the army, as long as there were still sons to tend to the household. Again, Incan households had big families.

When a woman married, she joined the household of her husband. But there are some records of laws indicating that women inherited land from their mother. Exactly how this worked is unclear, but it could be that the land she inherited went with her into the new household. See, most commoner did not live in the city. That was reserved for the nobility, the government, and the craftsmen who directly served the upper class. Commoners instead lived outside the city, in the farmlands, and a family could work several crops unconnected to their house. Regardless, this is yet another example of the Incans having a relative measure of equality between men and women.

Other jobs to be undertaken were that of a miner. Stones always needed to be quarried for building, and learning the art of perfectly fitting the building blocks together could take years to perfect. Mining for minerals and metals was also an important undertaking. To supply the upper class with the ornamentation their station so desired, miners uncovered gold, silver, copper, tin, and gemstones such as emerald and rose quartz.

In all, Inca society was fascinatingly unique. Moreover, it is so different from what many envision thanks to the common association between the Mayans and the Aztecs. Although human sacrifice did exist within the Inca Empire, it was practiced to a much lesser extent than the Mayans, and especially the Aztecs. On the other hand, despite the Incans apparent beliefs in equality, they never let a woman take the role of Sapa Inca, unlike both Mayans and Aztecs who had several female rulers over the course of history. So, too, should the Inca Empire be remembered as something different from the surrounding cultures of the time.

If it were not for the destruction of the recording system, both of the physical quipus and the knowledge of how to decipher them, we would know much more about the ins and outs of an everyday Incan's life. Much of it is conjecture, and some conflicting reports indicate that previous guesses may have been far off from the truth. There is no knowledge of how differing sexuality was viewed, or if the gender binary was as strictly enforced as we assume it to be. We know nothing about what the life of a princess would have entailed. The ongoing study into the history of the empire is the most we will ever get, but there is the hope that the science and technology of the future could provide a more in-depth look or a differing viewpoint.

Chapter 4: The Gods

Like most old-world civilizations, the Inca were polytheistic and worshipped a variety of gods. The foremost of these was Inti, the sun god. The Sapa Inca line was said to be descended from him, a claim made popular by Pachacuti. It was in the interest of keeping this bloodline pure that, by the 15th century, it was common practice for Incan royalty to wed brother to sister.

Apart from Inti, there were a vast array of gods, all of whom would be regularly sacrificed to. Llamas were the chosen animal for sacrifice, and lore dictated that different color coats signified which llamas were sacred to which god. White llamas, for example, were reserved for sacrifice to Inti.

Inti
The aforementioned chief god, and god of the sun. Many polytheistic cultures have a sun god as their central figure, given that the sun represents life-giving and creation. This is especially true for an agriculturally-based society like the Inca since the sun is needed for all main food sources to grow. Into was represented in art as a sun with a human face, wavy lines signifying his rays.

Solar eclipses were seen as the rare manifestation of Inti's anger. The sacrifice would increase, as a way to appease him. Since solar eclipses always end, the Inca believed their methods worked. He had many temples dedicated to him, the foremost of these was the Coricancha temple complex. Located in Cusco, it was the residence of the High Priest of the Sun, the Willaq Umu.

On the longest day of winter, when the sun was least in the sky, there was a great festival held in Inti's honor. As the Incan Empire resides in the Southern Hemisphere, this was on June 21. The festival, named Inti Raymi, would last several days past the solstice. It was common to see celebrators wearing gold sun masks representing Inti, and sacrifice to him would increase.

Pachamama
She was the great earth goddess. As the one who presided over the green earth and all its bounty, she also served as a fertility goddess. Today's representation of 'Mother Earth' owes much to her, as in Quechua, Pachamama literally means 'world mother.'

As one of the primary gods of the Incan religion, Pachamama was worshipped year-round. But during August, reverence to her increased. August, as the first month of spring, was the beginning of the sowing season. Prayers were sent up that the seeds would take root and the crops would be bountiful. A special ceremony was held on July 31: families would stay up all night, cooking until dawn. As the sun first drew over the horizon, a circle was dug into the dirt. If the soil that turned up was good and healthy, it promised a good year. A plate of food is them poured into a local river, and a prayer is said. Only then may the family eat.

In her anger, Pachamama would create the earthquakes. It was believed that if too much were taken from the earth, Pachamama would be weakened and angry and thusly retaliate. Thus, it was always important to the Inca that they were giving just as much to Pachamama as they took, and that they never took more than they needed.

Mama Quilla

This goddess of the moon was Pachamama's other child and Inti's sister-wife. She was the protector of women, marriage, and presided over the menstrual cycle. She cried tears made of silver, and so silver was sacred to her, and discs of silver would be used to represent her.

Because the moon was a cycle that could follow a month, Mama Quilla was seen as a timekeeper. Thus her godly duties extended to the calendar, and she was in charge of feast days and festivals. She also had several temples dedicated to her, all tended to faithfully by her priestesses.

Unlike her husband, Mama Quilla did not succumb to anger. Lunar eclipses were instead seen as an animal attacking her. Mama Quilla was incredibly beautiful, and every so often, an animal – be it a mountain lion, fox, snake, or something else – would fall madly in love with her and jump into the sky to be with her. The Incans, to save Mama Quilla, went out into the night to make noise, to try and scare the animal away. It was thought that, if the animal could not be frightened and the moon's light never returned, the world would be dark forever.

Illapa

Alongside Inti and Mama Quilla, this god was one of the three central gods of Incan religion. He reigned over the sky, the clouds, thunder and lightning, and rain. He was represented in art as a man, walking about the sky in a shining cloak, with a war club and sling in hand.

As the weather across the empire was so wild and important to agricultural output, Illapa was extremely important. He controlled the rain, and so could control when a drought would blight the land. He could also call up the great thunderstorm.

Lightning was his shining cloak, and the sound of thunder came from the crack of his sling.

He had a temple in Coricancha, tended to by his priests. His effigy within the temple had a headdress draped over his face, to represent clouds, veiling the storm and his anger.

Supay

Every polytheistic religion had a god of death, but the lengths to which they revered or feared this death dog varied widely. For the Inca, their death god came in the form of Supay, it was a fair and healthy mix of both.

The Inca world was divided into three spheres: the skies above where most of the gods resided, the earth where humans lived, and the land underground. This last realm, called Uku Pacha, was a place where the dead and demons resided. Supay was a hideous, gnarled, deformed figure, and he was said to come up to the mortal world in the form of a snake to watch over babies, wishing they would join him.

But how much of this bad reputation is true to Incan beliefs and how much was due to Catholic twisting is unclear. Whenever European settlers came into contact with a new polytheistic religion, they tried to equate it to their own beliefs. Thus Supay, like many other death gods before him, was equated with the Devil. This influence can be seen even today, where masks of him are portrayed with great devil horns.

The Andean people had an infamously high infant mortality rate, to the point that they did not even name children until their second birthday, so it is no wonder the story about Supay watching over children came to be. Believing that the god of death was fond of children and only wanted to take care of them was surely a way to help ease the pain of the death of a child.

Ekeko
When in need of good fortune, prayers would be sent to Ekeko. He was the god of prosperity, and predated the Inca Empire, receding all the way back to the Tiwanaku Empire. Always portrayed as smiling and with a smoke between his lips, Ekeko was truly a jolly god.

He is mostly presented in the form of an amulet, like a good luck token. Today, you are still likely to find a little statue of him kept in houses, as a way to bring good fortune to your family.

Chasca
Goddess of the dawn and twilight, patron of the morning and evening star, Chasca was also a goddess of beauty. She served as a protector of young girls before marriage.

The planet Venus, also known as the morning star and the evening star, is one of the planets visible to the naked eye. In almost every culture around the world, this star is associated with a goddess of the dawn, which usually symbolizes love and fertility on top. The Incans were no different. Chasca Was also associated with spring and renewal, so offerings to her would be filled with flowers.

Catequil
A complicated guy, Catequil was the god of thunder and lighting. Due to the much more prominent Illapa already being the god of storms, it was likely Catequil began as a local god from another tribe that joined the Inca Empire.

Incan mythology has little to no evidence of demigods, or children born from the union of a god and a mortal. The closest to this was the belief that the Sapa Inca was descended from Inti, but this was not believed to be due to a union with a mortal woman. Inti and Mama Quilla were the parents of Manco Capac, according to legend, and his mortality is unclear.

But there is some evidence to suggest that, where he was worshipped, Catequil was the father of all twins. The belief held that Catequil came to earth in the form of a lightning bolt and had relations with a mortal woman, and this resulted in twins. It is not known whether this belief was upheld all over the empire, or only in certain places. It makes one wonder what the rationale behind triplets was.

Pacha Kamaq
He began as a local god worshipped in the city-state of Pachacamac, by the Ichma people. Pacha Kamaq was their creator deity, and the city was named for him.

Like many small tribal gods, Pacha Kamaq was absorbed into the Incan pantheon when the state was merged with the empire. But what makes him noteworthy among the others is that Pacha Kamaq was raised to quite high importance. He was married to Pachamama. Sometimes he was portrayed as Inti's father, likely a confusion with another creator deity, Viracocha. Other portrayals have him as Inti's son. This confused placement within the pantheon signifies his origin in another place. It also highlights his popularity, and how the mythos attempted to insert him into such important positions.

Viracocha
The god of the skies and all creation. Initially, Viracocha was the primary deity worshipped by the Inca. But when Pachacuti

was crowned Sapa Inca, he promoted Inti to the position, and Viracocha gradually moved away from the focus.

But that is not to say that he didn't retain his importance. The story given was that he taught the first Andean people everything they needed to know, then retreated across the Pacific to spread knowledge to other cultures. As is the case with many disappearing religious figures, Viracocha promised to one day return.

Viracocha is widely regarded to have been the father of Inti and Mama Quilla, but there are some disputes. He remains mysterious, a name that was clearly important enough for the eights Sapa Inca – and Pachacuti's father himself – to have been named after him. Renderings of him in art strive to show his all-encompassing range and his importance over every other god, from wearing the sun as a crown, to the very rain being his tears. In each of his hands, he held a thunderbolt.

Mama Qucha
The goddess of the sea, patron to the fisherman. All creatures that lived beneath the waves were in her domain. She was the wife of Viracocha, and the mother of Inti and Mama Quilla.

But she was not only worshipped in the coastal regions. Mama Qucha was not the goddess of merely the sea, but of all bodies of water, fresh or salt. So lakes, rivers, and even man-made drainage channels were all under her domain.

What is truly amazing about Mama Qucha is that her sphere of influence tells us that the Incans understood the water cycle. They knew that runoff would return to the sea and that the same water would return to the clouds, and fall again as precipitation. For a society that had no scientific explorations and had not even use of the wheel, it is fascinating that a religious figure would help pass on such knowledge.

Alongside these, there were a variety of minor gods. Most of these minor deities, like Pacha Kamaq, were assimilated into the empire alongside their people. But worship for them remained fairly local. The Inca Empire was similar enough to the Roman Empire in this regard, never forcing a community to give up their own gods, only asking that the Incan gods also be worshipped, and held in highest regard.

Sacrifice

It's impossible to talk about any pre-Columbian religion without talking about one of their most sacred tenants: sacrifice. This was an unfortunate practice that no native Mesoamerican or South American civilization seems to have missed.

Though human sacrifice is found all over the world, it seems to be mostly associated today with the Mayans, the Aztecs, and the Inca. This is thanks to the Aztecs and their most extreme example of pulling out a human heart, a vivid image that doesn't leave the mind once it has entered. The Inca did not practice this, in particular, but rather had their own way of sacrificing.

Usually, when sacrifice is mentioned in this book, it means the sacrifice of food, drink, or personal items. These were the most common forms of sacrifice, and the ones practiced at every ritual. Animals were also common, mostly the abundant llama. But the Incans did engage in something they called 'Qhapaq Hucha,' and it was a form of child sacrifice.

The practice was rationalized as the Incans sending their best children to join the gods. The chosen were drugged with a combination of coca leaves and chicha, an alcoholic beverage. These children, who were well-fed before the sacrificial walk beforehand to ensure their happiness, were sent to the highest point on the mountains they could reach. They were sent with the finest clothing, jewels and other artifacts, and more delicious food. They would die on the mountains.

The weather conditions of the Andes have led to the discovery of mummified children in the mountainous peaks. These include Momia Juanita, whose body is on display at the Museo Santuarios Andinos in Peru. But most famous of these is the perfectly preserved 14-year-old girl known only as The Maiden. Her body sits at the High Mountain Archaeological Museum in Argentina. Despite the sadness that comes with finding such bodies, their mummified state allowed anthropologists and historians to learn new things about Incan society.

Unlike the future Spaniards, the Incan war was never really driven by religious movement. When the empire did go to war, it was usually because their treaty negotiations didn't work.

War Boys
One of the notable points of interest about Incan battle tactics was their tendency to peacock. Even after marching an army all the way to a destination, Incans would try to impress their enemies into submission with displays of strength. In a way, this is just another part of their negotiations. Pachacuti's style of enticing others to join the empire relied on assuring the outside force that their state would only benefit from making the decision. By displaying such military power, the Incans were assuring their enemies that this was the power they could be a part of. They did not have to fight, but could instead

choose to be on the winning side. It is not known how often this succeeded, but it clearly did not work every time.

When they were called to battle, the Incan armies employed tactics, not unlike those found in other early armies. The militia was divided into subsections based on weapons used. First, the projectile division would rain down spears and stones on the enemy, softening their ranks. After this, the first line would march, consisting of men with battering weapons. Most commonly used were war clubs, or a kind of mace called a macana.

While the front lines engaged the opposing army in hand to hand combat, back divisions would split apart and circle around the opposing army. These separate division would then hit the flanks, pushing the enemy in on all sides and effectively encircling them. Surrender came from the enemy generals soon after.

The Inca also had a habit of employing psychological warfare in their battles. After a show of peacocking, they would advance to the front lines of the battlefield in complete, eerie silence. Once the armies were in place, the Inca would erupt in a mass of jeering and catcalls. This could quite often unsteady their opponents, causing them to lose faith in themselves, or subconsciously believe that the Inca were unbeatable and the war was effectively already lost.

The Incans did not have a prominent god of war, showing how they were not a military-based civilization. Still, despite this, they were largely undefeated in battle. Tactics combined with the sheer mass of soldiers meant they would be at an advantage against any foe. That is, any foe native to their land.

Chapter 5: Decline and Downfall

So how did an empire so vast and so strong crumble to pieces within such a short period of time? It is often touted that Rome did not fall in a day, but the Inca Empire certainly seems to have. Surely, the invading force of a foreign nation and one with lesser numbers on top of that could not be solely responsible for such a devastation. And, partially, this is true. The Inca Empire was already beginning to fracture by the time the Spanish made contact. And there were more factors at play when it came to the invading army, more than just size. Advanced technology, weaponry, mass plague, and even understanding of the stars all contributed to the near-instant takeover of the glorious empire.

Civil War

Anytime a dynasty is based on a royal bloodline, a war for succession is guaranteed to break out. The Inca Empire was no different. The line of Pachacuti began to crumble in 1527, upon the death of his grandson, Huayna Capac.

Like most Sapa Inca before him, Huayna Capac was married to his full-blooded sister, Coya Cusirimay. As is often the case with incestuous unions, the couple had trouble conceiving, and this left him with no sons born by his royal wife. They did have daughters, but none of them could be considered heirs. The title of Sapa Inca had never been, and would never be, bestowed to a woman.

Huayna Capac, however, was known for his multiple affairs and produced some 50 illegitimate sons with a variety of other women. Still, none of these sons could inherit. Eventually, Coya

Cusirimay was set aside. Huayna Capac took his younger sister, Rahua Ocllo. Finally, he had a trueborn son and heir, Ninan Cuyochi.

But death lingered on the horizon for this family. In 1526, the Spanish conquerors were making their way south in search of greater riches. Huayna Capac traveled to meet them, and though this delegation was peaceful in nature, the great Sapa Inca contracted smallpox. That small moment of interaction was all it took to send a dynasty crumbling. Huayna Capac died shortly after, alongside his brother – and his heir, Ninan Cuyochi.

With his sudden death, Huayna Capac had left no instructions for the line of succession. The Incans were unprepared for a situation like this, and it was unclear to whom the title should pass. Two choices were put forward. The first was Huascar, the younger brother of Ninan Cuyochi, born to the royal wife, Rahua Ocllo. The second option was Atahualpa, one of Huayna's illegitimate sons.

The nobility backed Huascar, the only option in their eyes. He was pure of blood, the rightful heir. Atahualpa, however, would have been the political choice. For during Huayna Capac's reign, he had continued the legacy of his father and grandfather by expanding and conquering new territory. The most prominent of these acquisitions was the northern province of Quito. Atahualpa's mother was a member of the demoted royal family. Thus, Atahualpa was beloved among the northern regions as a man of their people. He had also, in the years leading up to his father's death, gained popularity among the rest of the empire for being personable, intelligent, and dignified.

In an attempt to appease the common people, Atahualpa was sent to his homeland in the north to be a kind of governor. Huascar was crowned Sapa Inca. But this tentative peace could not last long. Huascar, unsecured in his place on the throne, began to fear that his half-brother would rise up against him. He demanded all his subjects pay tribute. Now, Atahualpa was more than happy and sent the newly crowned Sapa Inca tributes and messengers to extoll his loyalty. But Huascar, who was growing increasingly paranoid, saw this all as a trick. He murdered the messengers and sent them back, becoming a self-fulfilling prophecy as Atahualpa then declared war.

The following five years saw the empire ravaged with battle. Atahualpa and his forces descended south, encountering victory in almost every battle. Near 1533, Atahualpa's generals reached Cusco and seized the city. Huascar and his family were seized and killed.

This might have seen the end of the war, and the empire might have gradually returned to peace and stabilization after this. But within that five-year span, the Spanish explorers had returned to the Spanish-conquered cities in Central America, with reports of the vast wealth the city of Cusco. The Spanish army obtained a seal from the emperor, Charles I, ordering them to conquer the Incans in the name of the Spanish Empire. So the armies returned, under the leadership of conquistador Francisco Pizarro.

New Castile
Francisco Pizarro had been living in the impoverished Panama region, and it was the promise of these richer lands down south that first spurred him onward. Though the previous quest into the Andes never reached the city of Cusco, the rumors he heard were enough for him to petition a return with reinforcements.

Upon Pizarro's return, he came across Atahualpa. Pizarro's men and their customs scared Atahualpa, and he did not know whether to drive them away or welcome them. He wasn't given much time to deliberate, because the Spanish captured him shortly afterward. While Atahualpa's men killed Huascar elsewhere, Atahualpa himself was executed.

An example of Pizarro's cunning and cruelty can be seen during Atahualpa's imprisonment. Atahualpa promised Pizarro a room full of gold for ransom if he would release him. Pizarro agreed, and the gold was delivered. Pizarro had no intention of ever releasing Atahualpa but continued to promise, allowing the gold and silver to pile up. In his greed, he wanted to keep Atahualpa alive so the riches would keep coming. But his men demanded the execution, and so eventually Pizarro complied.

The Incan Empire had already suffered one succession crisis that led to the civil war and now faced another. As the Spanish took advantage of the weakened defenses, they entered Cusco and placed Yupanqui, the younger brother of Atahualpa, on the throne.

Much of the nobility saw the Spanish as liberators, here to put an end to the civil war and restore peace to their empire. They welcomed the Spanish and celebrated their new Sapa Inca. But what the nobles did not realize at first was that Yupanqui was nothing but a puppet, a face Pizarro could put on the throne to earn the loyalty of the native people. In practice, the Inca Empire was now under the complete control of Pizarro. In the grand tradition of renaming native regions 'New' Christian city, the area was dubbed New Castile. As governor, Pizarro was tasked to give the state a new capital, to which he chose a coastal city and renamed in Lima. Now, hundreds of Spanish would pour in, taking the land for themselves and settling amongst the natives.

A Rebel with a Cause
In 1535, Pizarro left Cusco to chase one of the last remaining forces of resistance. His brothers, Juan and Gonzalo, were left behind alongside Yupanqui to maintain control. This would prove to be a mistake, as the two brothers mistreated Yupanqui. The Sapa Inca came to realize the lack of power he held in his position, and that the once-revered title had become an in-name-only clause. With only two guards on him, Yupanqui escaped into the surrounding highlands.

Now seeing the Spanish for what they truly were, Yupanqui rallied the people behind him. Spending ten months on the run, as a kind of mythical exiled prince, Yupanqui took smaller cities and eliminated small Spanish outposts. He returned to Cusco a year later with a new army behind him. At the same time, his close general and possible brother, Quiso, led a siege on the city of Lima. Both were successful. Yupanqui even managed to repel four entire reinforcement squads, until Pizarro himself was forced to return to deal with Yupanqui himself.

Pizarro's forces retook Cusco with some ease, and Yupanqui retreated to Vilcabamba, a small post in the eastern jungles of Antisuyu. He took everyone he could, from his royal family to commoners, and settled within the trees. Those around him at the time said Yupanqui considered this his final defeat, and did the best he could to turn this little settlement into the new seat for the Inca Empire. Never again would he attempt to retake his old lands.

Vilcabamba became known as the New-Inca, or New Inca kingdom, but it only lasted 33 years before it, too, was overtaken by the Spaniards. With that, the last remaining independence of the Inca Empire was snuffed out.

Steel vs. Bronze

The level of technological differences between the two forces cannot be stressed enough. During the 16th century, the Incans were still using bronze and stone weapons. They had never needed a reason to advance their weaponry. Much of Incan expansion was done through the use of political maneuvering, and when war between tribes did occur, the opposing forces used bronze and stone as well.

But by this point in time, Europe had been through countless crusades. The process of alloying iron and carbon to create steel had been perfected by everyone from the Vikings to the Indians, and it was the common metal found in weapons. The use of gunpowder from China had spread to every corner of the Eastern Hemisphere. Spain itself had lived through the Reconquista, a campaign that lasted almost 800 years.

Bronze is an alloy of copper and tin. Both of these are members of the seven metals of antiquity, metals mostly used by the ancient world. As others, both copper and tin are fairly soft and malleable. When forged together to create bronze, they are stronger than iron. Bronze was a reliable metal and had its many uses outside weaponry. But to put it in perspective, the Bronze Age ended in the year 300 – B.C.E.

Steel, on the other hand, alloys iron with carbon. Iron is a far more abundant metal than tin, and carbon could be found in a variety of places. Steel has a higher durability and is less likely to shatter upon impact. It retains an edge for longer, meaning less time is needed to maintain the upkeep of a blade. Spanish rapiers, in particular, were known for their incredible bend.

When Francisco Pizarro and his men arrived on the Andes frontier, he had one cannon, 27 horses, and 168 men at his back. Each of these men had a steel sword, steel armor, and a gun. No matter how many Incan soldiers swarmed the men, they were hopelessly outmatched. Their bolas, the stone-throwing weapons that had served head injuries for centuries, could hardly make a dent in the helmets of their adversaries.

It is also important to note that, as is so often forgotten, horses are not native to the Americas. The Incans would never have seen something like them before. The llamas and other camelids of their homelands were not large or strong enough to support a rider, so the Incan infantry had never included mounted soldiers. There were no known strategies for defending against such a force.

Bending the Gods
The Reconquista and the subsequent conquering of the New World were backed by an unwavering religious belief. The Spanish were strong in their beliefs that Christianity should be the only religion. Before it was an empire, Spain had been under the control of the Islamic Empire, and the Reconquista was the long-fought process to expel all Muslim influence and insert absolute Christian authority.

As the Spaniards assumed control of the Inca Empire, they too the native pantheon and merged it with their own beliefs. Hence Supay became the Devil, Pachamama was the Virgin Mary, and Viracocha was the closest they had to God. This practice was common for all invading Christians, and almost every pagan religion has these influences that are still seen today.

One of the ways the Spaniards dazzled the Incans was with their knowledge of astronomy. Because they could predict when lunar eclipses would happen, priests considered them in the highest regard. It is a bit of a misconception that the Spanish annihilated the natives in a bloodbath. Their takeover was much more insidious. The newcomers were welcomed, even celebrated. Between their puppet rulers, baptisms, and intermarriages, the Spanish Empire had successfully absorbed the Inca Empire.

The Plagues

Alongside smallpox, the Spanish brought a whole host of disease that the native people's immune systems had no resistance to and no way of fighting. Typhus, measles, and the flu were three of the other most common offenders. Though most of these diseases are treatable, to the unprepared body, they were instantly fatal.

Human immune systems build resistance to bacterial infections over time. Today, immunization is achieved by inserting dead bacterial cells into the bloodstream, so white blood cells learn to recognize the disease and fight it. The native people of the Americas had no time to build an immune system. Although these diseases were just as dangerous to the Spanish and the conquistadors suffered an immense number of fatalities, it was nothing compared to the effect it had on the native population.

The diseases were not just carried to the Incans by the newcomers. Plagues had already devastated 90% of the

Mesoamerican population and were now spreading south independent of the relatively small Spanish army.

If the succession crisis hadn't happened, and the Inca Empire was united under Atahualpa, perhaps the invasion would have played out differently. But while the ravaging of the civil war certainly made things easier, in the end, it's likely it wouldn't have mattered. Between war, plague, and advanced technology, the Andean people were almost completely wiped out. Along with their knowledge of the quipu went agricultural knowledge and local religions. In just a few short years, the Inca Empire had gone from one of the richest and far-reaching empires of the Western Hemisphere to near extinction.

Chapter 6: Remains of the Day

With so much creativity, color, and ingenious architecture lost to the ages, it would be easy to think that the only thing that remains of the great Inca Empire is the ruins of the city of Machu Picchu. But besides that marvel, there are so many little things the Incans left behind. Things that influence us even today, things that you might not even think to attribute to them.

Machu Picchu
Lost to the heights of the Andes after the conquest, the city of Machu Picchu was only rediscovered in 1911. Thanks to much of the destruction of classical architecture by the Spanish, it was Machu Picchu that showed the world just how precise the Inca were with their building techniques. Machu Picchu shocked the world with its beauty, splendor, and structural integrity.

Though the origins of Machu Picchu are unknown, it is widely regarded to have been commissioned by Pachacuti as a summer retreat, as a kind of vacation palace, for the royal family. It has remains of living quarters along with a temple for the god Inti and terraced fields for agriculture.

At an altitude of 2,400 meters above sea level, the existence of Machu Picchu as a vacation palace truly puts into perspective how incredible the evolutionary adaptations of the Andean people truly were. The hike to Machu Picchu today is dangerous, and many suffer from altitude sickness while trying to visit. Some with blood pressure conditions may never even get a chance to see the city, as their doctors would strongly advise against it.

But despite the conditions, for its beauty and its look into Incan architecture, Machu Picchu is the center of Peruvian tourism. The city has boosted the economy, providing the country one of its largest sources of revenue. It is also a named World Heritage Site and was recently chosen as one of the New Seven Wonders of the World.

Machu Picchu is the grandest, but not the only surviving bit of monumental Incan architecture. The Coricancha Temple in Cusco remains are fairly well-preserved, and another key part of Peru's tourism industry. Those on their way to Machu Picchu usually begin in Cusco, following the same ascent as Pachacuti and his family would have done.

Food
Many of your favourite foods to this day are likely Incan in origin. Chili peppers originate from all over the Americas, but the Inca was one of the reasons their cultivation became so common. Columbus, for all his many flaws, did manage to introduce the chili pepper to Europe.

Chicha is an alcoholic beverage fermented mostly from maize. It was the staple alcohol of the Inca, and the drink usually poured in sacrifice to the gods. It is still a popular drink to this day, and its origins have not been forgotten.

The reason we associate pumpkins and other squash with Thanksgiving is actually thanks to the Inca and other Mesoamerican civilizations. Because the squash was such an integral part of their diet, and so foreign to Columbus and his men, the imaginary image of the Thanksgiving meal between pilgrims and natives included these foods as a key component. The next time you take a slice of pumpkin pie, give thanks to the Inca.

We talked about the coca leaf and its negative effects in creating the drug cocaine. But when the soda brand Coca-Cola was founded in 1886, the two things they used to create their signature flavor was kola nuts and coca leaves. Though cola leaves are not part of the secret recipe anymore, without the Inca chewing these leaves, we wouldn't have Coke as we know it today. Perhaps because of its origin, Coke is especially popular in Central and South America today.

Language
The Quechua language is still spoken by natives in the Andean regions today, meaning that although the quipus are a lost art, not all methods of communication are gone.

It is a miracle that the language survived for all the years it did. During the 18th century and the height of Spanish occupancy, Quechua was suppressed and speaking it became outlawed. But it was the Spanish themselves who allowed the Quechuan languages to continue. Back in their earlier days of supremacy, missionaries encouraged the learning of Quechua, to better communicate with the native people. In fact, it was a Spaniard himself, Domingo de Santo Tomas, who first began to record Quechua in the Latin alphabet. He is most likely the reason we can read it today.

Thanks to the division of the Inca Empire, the Quechua languages split into two branches, known simply as Quechua I and Quechua II. The differences between these come down to the local dialect. Quechua I, also known as Central Quechuan, has speakers mostly grouped around the center of the Andes, as the name would suggest. It remains fairly uniform as all the speakers a geographically close together. Quechua II, also known as Peripheral Quechuan, is the dialect spoken in the farther reaches. Because it is so widely distributed, there are several subdivisions within the language. Some of these differences can get quite drastic. And yet, Quechuan speakers of all dialects can understand one another through the differences.

Quechua has managed to survive and to this day is spoken by more than 8 million people. It is the largest surviving language of the native Americas and is an official language of Peru and Bolivia. You can even hear it in blockbuster movies. *Star Wars* and its famous character, Greedo, used Quechuan as the basis for his alien language. The fourth *Indiana Jones* movie, which partly takes place in South America, has the famed hero speaking Quechuan with native Peruvians. And in a notable example, the Quechuan name Tupac has risen to fame today thanks to famed rapper and entertainer, Tupac Shakur.

Inti Raymi
One of the great Incan gods has not been forgotten. Inti, their most important god of the sun, has experienced a revival, especially in regards to his yearly festival. Inti Raymi has become a national holiday of Peru. Just like in the days of the Empire, the nine-day celebration begins on June 24.

If you want to witness this event today, all you need to do is visit Peru during your summer vacation. The parades in the city of Cusco are so vibrant that half the city is shut down. What is truly special about today's Inti Raymi, as well, is the regard to which it holds the native people. Dancers, singers, and entertainers from the four Incan regions are part of the procession. Every year, two Quechuan actors are chosen to portray the Sapa Inca, Manco Capac, and his consort, Mama Ocllo.

Entertainers and overseers alike dress in traditional clothing. The procession hen follows the same path it did 600 years ago when Pachacuti was the Sapa Inca. Beginning at the heart of Cusco at the Coricancha Temple, it follows all the way to the ruins of Sacsayhuaman on the outskirts of the city. Libations are poured out as a sacrifice, to honor the great god Inti. In our modern day, the celebrator is likely honoring the great people who came before them.

The actor portraying the Sapa Inca, at exactly 1:30 PM, gives a speech to the surrounding crown, and another to the watching Inti. Beer is passed around, performances are held, and the festival once again kicks into party mode.

The Goddess Cult of Pachamama

From the 1960s onward, the rising movements of Neopaganism and feminism coalesced to create a kind of modern cult that was strictly goddess-based. This modern religion has no rulebook, guidelines, or even a name, but it is used by many women who dabble in spiritualism, occultism, and naturalism. Though often parodied, such as in the 1994 hit sitcom *Friends* with its book 'Be Your Own Wind-Keeper,' the actual goddess cults of modern day are quite down to earth.

Rooted in the feminist movement and the art of building self-esteem, goddess cultism is like astrology. Believers can range anywhere from passing fancies to devoted students. Most members are just women who enjoy researching the women of the pagan pantheons. Usually stemming from a childhood fascination with a figurehead like Artemis or Freya, research into a variety of pre-Christian mythical women leads many women to direct their prayers to a patron goddess or two.

But for the New Age movement of South America, interest in the earth goddess Pachamama has increased more than almost any other. Her conflagration with the Virgin Mary means that many mestizo Andeans – that is, Andeans with mixed white and native heritage – are simultaneously Christians and pagan goddess worshippers. Interest in Pachamama has peaked across the world, and tourist guides often enthuse visitors to sacrifice drink or small items to Pachamama while in sacred sites, such as Machu Picchu. The practice is very similar to the tourism of Hawaii, which uses sacrifice to the volcano goddess Pele as a part of visiting the Kilauea crater.

Like Inti, Pachamama has her own festival today in Peru and Ecuador, known as Pachamama Raymi. Held on August 1, the festival is not quite so large as Inti Raymi, but that fact that worship of her survives is nevertheless a sign that not all of the Inca Empire is lost to the ages.

Conclusion

The tragic loss of the Inca Empire on the rest of the world cannot be overstated enough. So much culture and knowledge was lost and was doomed to be since the day Christopher Columbus set out to sea. And yet, in the face of so much adversity, some has remained to this day.

The grand history of the Andean people, from their humble beginnings to the height and glory of an ever-reaching empire, is almost too fantastic to be real. Through innovation and determination, the Andeans overcame great odds to call those Andes home. Evolutionary adaptations the likes of which can't be found in any other civilization mark the Inca as unique.

Their pantheon is fascinating and deserves the same level of study given to the Greek Olympians or the comic book featuring Norse gods. Their policy of acquiring new territory through negotiations and mutually beneficial deals, and the respect to which they showed such territories, are the kind of politics we should be adapting to fit our modern values. They should never be confused for the Mayans or the Aztecs, nor should they be touted as copycats or an offshoot that came afterward. The Inca were proud, independent, hardworking, loyal, and strong. Honor their memory by understanding them, learning their history, and sharing the knowledge with everyone you can. Visit Peru, take part in Inti Raymi and Pachamama Raymi.

And the next time you have a Coca-Cola, pour one out for the glory of the Inca Empire.

www.ingramcontent.com/pod-product-compliance
Lightning Source LLC
Chambersburg PA
CBHW052208110526
44591CB00012B/2123